The Power of Attraction   Steven Claysen

THE POWER OF ATTRACTION

HOW TO APPLY THE LAW OF ATTRACTION TO CREATE THE LIFE YOU WANT

BY STEVEN CLAYSEN

The Power of Attraction   Steven Claysen

First Edition published 2015
Second Edition published 2016

ISBN-13: 978-0-9852470-9-6
ISBN-10: 098524096

White Horse Books
www.whitehorselibrary.com

Cover Design by Connie Gorton

Cover photograph by Charles Uibel

See more of Charles Uibel's work at:
http://greatsaltlake.photography/

"Ask yourself what is really important. Have the wisdom and courage to build your life around your answer."

– Lee Jampolsky

Table of Contents

Author's Note:

I want to thank you and congratulate you for purchasing *"The Power of Attraction: How to Apply the Law of Attraction to Create the Life You Want"*.

You may not realize it but you are already using the power of the Law of Attraction to create the life you are living. If any aspect of your life isn't what you hoped it would be, then this book can help you.

"The Power of Attraction" contains proven steps and strategies on how to create the life you want through practical application of the Law of Attraction. This book will show you how to apply the Law of Attraction to help you attain the positive things you are looking for; relationships, circumstances, prosperity, joy, etc.

As this is a book about *doing*, I have included a number of exercises which will require you to do some writing. *I suggest you have a special notebook for writing your responses to the exercises* contained herein.

Thanks again for purchasing this book. May it bring you all the joy that you are seeking!

9

CHAPTER ONE

THE POWER OF CHOICE

All of us have been given a powerful gift.

It is the gift of *freewill;* the ability to choose our beliefs, thoughts, feelings and actions. It is referred to as the free independence of mind which has been so graciously bestowed upon the human family as one of its choicest gifts.

We must be careful not to confuse freewill with freedom. When we refer to freewill we refer to an exercise of the will, the Power of Choice. When we refer to freedom, we mean the power and privilege to carry out our choices. This includes everything from thoughts, such as love or hate, to actions, such as running or walking.

Freewill, the Power of Choice, is a gift. You have the power and privilege to act for yourself. Because of this, no person or organization can take away your freewill in this life.

What *can* be taken away or reduced by the conditions of life is your freedom, or the power to act upon your choices. Freewill is absolute; but in the circumstances of our mortal existence, freedom is always qualified.

Freewill, which we all have, is the ability to choose our own beliefs, our own thoughts, our own feelings and our own actions. These choices create for each of us our own personal reality. Our future is under our personal control and not at the mercy of some uncertain or capricious external influence.

Your ability and power to choose your own thoughts, to impress ideas into your subconscious mind, to visualize your dreams and desires is what ultimately puts you in control of your own life. You get to choose.

Freewill is your power to become. Every choice you make moves you closer toward or further from what you are meant to become.

While it is true that you may freely choose what you think, it is also true that you are *not* free from the consequences of your thoughts. The result of your thought is governed by an immutable law.

Thought results in action.

If your thoughts are constructive, if they are harmonious and peaceful, the consequences of your mental processes will be positive. If your thoughts are destructive, however, the results of your thinking will be destructive.

"The best way to predict the future is to create it."

\- Peter Drucker

Thought is a powerful tool. Any thought you persist in will eventually produce its result in the nature, health, and circumstances of your life. This places you in a powerful position! Your power simply needs to be unfolded, developed and cultivated to become a useful tool in creating the world of your desires.

The Law of Attraction will definitely and accurately bring you the conditions, environment, and experiences in life that correspond with your habitual, typical, and predominant thought patterns.

Successful people make it their business to hold ideals for the conditions they wish to manifest in their world. They constantly and consistently think on the next step necessary in the achievement of the ideal for which they are striving.

Their thoughts are the tools and their imagination is the material they use to build successful lives. Thought is the force they use to build their successes; imagination is the matrix in which their world is fashioned.

The ideal held steadily in your thoughts is what predetermines and *attracts* the conditions necessary for its fulfilment in your success as well. If you are faithful to your ideal, circumstances will materialize for its manifestation. The results will correspond in exact ratio to your fidelity to that ideal.

I know a man who hates his job. He is determined to find something better for himself, yet every day he focuses on how terrible his situation is. Every day he concentrates on how unfair his employer treats him. He determined to be out of that career in five years and yet it has been sixteen years now and still he continues in the same job, in the same situation, with the same complaints.

I know a woman who hated her job. Every day she focused on what her dream job would look like. Every day she visualized herself working under pleasant conditions with a kinder supervisor. Within six months she found herself in a better position, with better supervisors and increased wages.

Your conceptual reality is the result of your continuous method of thinking. The circumstances of your life are a direct manifestation of the quality of your thoughts. The quality and consistency of your thoughts is the cause of all the circumstances, whether good or bad, you are experiencing in your life at this moment.

Exercise 1.1:

What are the conditions you wish to manifest in your life?

Identify at least 3 areas of your life you would like to improve through conscious effort and the exercise of freewill. Write them in your notebook. (See *Author's Note* on page 9 of this book.)

Your thoughts construct the mold from which your future will emerge.

It is the focus of your thoughts and the exercise of your freewill in choosing empowering thoughts that creates your material world. What you focus your thoughts on becomes your reality.

So what are you focusing on? Is it positive or is it negative? Listen to your thoughts. What are you thinking? Where is your attention and focus? Concentrate your thought only on the conditions that you desire to create for yourself and for others.

Exercise 1.2:

Think of the three areas of your life you would like to improve.

Identify the habitual or undirected thoughts that are creating the difficulties you are experiencing in these three areas. Write these thoughts in your notebook.

Ignore, forget and reject all thoughts of conditions you do not wish to create. Do not give negative thoughts power. If you refuse to pay attention to thoughts of conditions you do not want and focus your attention entirely on what you do what, you will be empowered to create the life of your dreams.

You cannot create the life you want by thinking about the life you do not want any more than you can describe light by talking about darkness. You do not create what you want by thinking about what you don't want.

You will not achieve peace by saying that war is bad. You achieve peace by being peaceful. You will not achieve wealth by hating poverty. You achieve wealth by becoming abundant. You will never find love by despising hate. You will find love by being more loving.

You will not achieve anything in your life by thinking about its opposite. You achieve by focusing all of your thoughts, beliefs, feelings, and actions on that which you desire.

It is a constant and natural law that like begets like. Your thoughts, your dreams and your ideals will attract into your outer world exactly what you focus on in your inner world—your mental world.

Exercise 1.3:

Identify the negative thoughts you need to eliminate and replace in order to achieve the circumstances you wish to create.

What new thoughts will you create to replace these old negative thoughts? Write at least three empowering thoughts in your notebook that correspond with the three areas of your life that you wish to improve.

The power of the Law of Attraction is no secret. It is the power of love. Love creates. Love binds. Love is powerful energy.

One expression of love is desire. Attach desire to any thought and believe in its reality and it will manifest itself.

Every thought, every feeling, every action you take causes a reaction. You are at cause. You have this power within you. You use it constantly, either deliberately with deliberate results or unintentionally with unintended and random results.

Thinking is an act of creation. Everything that exists in our physical world began in the mind as a concept.

Pain and suffering are a result of your thoughts and feelings not being in harmony with what you desire. Harmony in your thinking will create harmony in your life. Peaceful thoughts will create a peaceful world.

Seeing the world around you as a reflection of your thoughts, as a mirror of what takes place in your mind, will allow you to understand that in order to change your world, you must first change yourself.

To change yourself you must simply exercise your Power of Choice, your freewill, to change your thoughts, change your beliefs, change your feelings, and change your actions.

Your life does not control you.

You control your life.

You are free to create for yourself an entirely new reality by consciously choosing what to think and believe and then selecting data to input into your mind that supports your new belief.

If you exercise your Power of Choice, to choose your beliefs and thoughts, information will be *attracted* to support those thoughts and beliefs. If you exercise your freewill to choose your purpose and goals, and attach a desire to receiving them, then things, circumstances, people, and ideas will be attracted to support and fulfill them.

Most people do not understand that their mental ability to attract is under their conscious control and therefore they unintentionally attract what they unconsciously think and believe.

The use of your freewill to originate a thought, a belief, a feeling, or an action is what allows you to create your own circumstance and not become a creature of circumstance. Everything that exists in your real world began at one point as a thought in your mental world.

You have freewill. You can choose to have conscious control over your thoughts, feelings, beliefs and actions. It is not just artists and inventors who use this creative ability. Everyone does it all the time, although most people do not realize that this process is under their conscious control.

So remember, even if you are not doing it, you are doing it. You can remake your entire reality by a simple conscious choice to take control and exercise your freewill.

Every thought is a choice. Every emotion is a choice. Most people allow previous experience and present conditions to determine their feelings and thoughts. They end up being controlled.

When you exercise your freedom of choice, you are in control. Conscious choice produces results in harmony with your desires. Intention and conscious choice enable you to be a creator of circumstance instead of being a creature of circumstance.

You can become more by the conscious choice of how you think, what you believe, how you feel and what you say and do.

A practical understanding of the Power of Choice will substitute wealth for poverty, wisdom for ignorance, harmony for discord and freedom for oppression.

"Happiness is a choice, not a result. Nothing will make you happy until you choose to be happy."

-- Ralph Marston

Your personal power is determined by your personal choices. The circumstances of your life are directly under your own control. By learning to understand and control the Power of Choice, you will develop the ability to create for yourself the life of your dreams.

The choice is yours.

CHAPTER TWO

THE POWER OF CONSCIOUSNESS

Here is a simple yet powerful experiment. Look in a mirror. Describe what you see.

Now ask yourself, "Am I that body? Is that really who I am?" Or are you simply your mind perceiving your body? The question is imponderable to many people and consequently they simply ignore it altogether. However, if you want to understand who you are in order to maximize your relationship to life, it is necessary to understand the answer.

"The sky isn't the limit; the mind that sees the sky is the limit."

– Byron Kafic

Look in the mirror again. If you were to lose a hand or a foot or an arm, would that still be you in the mirror? Absolutely!

You are obviously not just your body. There is more to you than just the physical you.

You are not just your mind either. There is something more and far greater to who you are. There is a pervasive force in the universe, a universal intelligence that is in everything and everywhere. This all-encompassing element is individualized in you and in all sentient beings.

Your consciousness does not just reside in your body. It does not just reside in your brain. Your consciousness exists within this vast universal intelligence. Your consciousness uses your body as a vehicle. It uses your mind for expression.

LIVE LESS OUT OF HABIT AND MORE OUT OF INTENT.

Your consciousness, this quality of being aware of something, is found within. It is your consciousness that uses the power of freewill to make the choices which create your life and your world.

The only power your consciousness currently possesses is the power to think. The expression, *"as a man thinketh in his heart, so is he,"* becomes even more significant as our understanding of our consciousness increases. What you think is what you are.

The all-important question now becomes; "Just what are you thinking?"

Is there purpose to your thoughts or are your thoughts just random streams of consciousness floating like driftwood on the seas of your mind? Are your thoughts constructive? Are they purposeful and deliberate or are they merely replaying all the old programming of your childhood?

Listen carefully.

"Dream lofty dreams, and as you dream, so shall you become."

– James Allen

There is a vast difference between simply thinking and actually directing your thoughts consciously, systematically, and constructively. Thought is creative and will automatically correlate with the object of your thinking and bring it into manifestation.

Listen very carefully to the thoughts running through your mind. If you are like most people, the majority of your thinking consists of negative input or totally useless chatter.

Examine your thinking pattern. You will discover that the continuous flow of thoughts coursing through your mind is just like a looped tape recording running endlessly, replaying over and over the same useless and unproductive ideas.

The input you have received over the years, especially during your formative childhood years, has mostly been limiting in nature and non-supportive of what you truly want in life. And your mind simply continues to replay this old information over and over and over again.

YOUR CONCEPTUAL REALITY IS THE RESULT OF YOUR ON-GOING METHOD OF THINKING.

Since your thoughts are the determining factor in creating your life and your world at this very moment, and since your thoughts are under your own conscious control through the gift of freewill, then why not CHOOSE to THINK thoughts which contribute to your personal happiness, to your physical health, and to your abundant wealth?

But how do you replace these old tapes? The brain simply doesn't come with an eject button.

The truth is you can't replace them but you can record over them. Affirm in your mind what you want until it erases and replaces your old programming with a newer, stronger, and more powerful belief program. The greatest power we possess is the power to think, but few of us know how to think constructively or correctly and, consequently, we achieve only mediocre or indifferent results.

Thinking is a spiritual, creative activity. Thinking creates electrochemical processes in the brain. The brain physically records those thoughts. The more a thought is repeated, with an emotional attachment such as desire, a stronger thought pattern is created. As more brain cells are locked into that thought pattern, a permanent record is formed which becomes a belief.

When enough of your brain has become impressed with this belief, it becomes a part of who you are. Your words and actions and the attendant results will follow. You become whatever you choose to become by choosing first what you think about. *You are what you think.* The effect you produce in your world is the direct result of the action and re-action known as thinking.

Every thought sets brain cells in action and your thoughts are the cause of your reality. You have constructed the entire experience of your life and you continue to do so every moment of every day.

The mind is a complex and wondrous tool. Like any tool, it can be used or misused. A hammer and chisel can be used by an unskilled laborer to take down a wall or it can be used by a genius like Michelangelo to create the statue of David. Likewise, the mind can be used destructively or it can be used elegantly.

Your mind's first attribute is passive; it is a recording device. It takes in everything it is exposed to and replays any part when asked or stimulated to do so. The mind's second attribute is active and has three faculties; interpretation, attraction, and creation.

Your mind's ability to *interpret* information allows you to discriminate between qualities like up or down, light or dark, good or bad, etc. It gives you the Power of Choice to determine what is important to you and what is meaningless. It also allows you to decide what your reality is.

Your mind's ability to interpret is under your conscious control. Whenever you decide that something is true and choose to believe it, everything you see or hear is perceived as supporting that belief. Once you accept that *your reality is based on your perception,* then you are free to choose a new reality by consciously choosing to think and believe differently.

THERE IS A VAST DIFFERENCE BETWEEN SIMPLY THINKING AND ACTUALLY DIRECTING OUR THOUGHTS CONSCIOUSLY, SYSTEMATICALLY AND CONSTRUCTIVELY.

The mind's ability to *attract* operates all the time, but it is also under your conscious control. Most people do not understand this and they attract what they unconsciously think and believe, the negative and limiting thoughts of their past as previously programmed by the recording function of the mind. If you choose new beliefs and thoughts, new information will be attracted to support them.

Your mind's ability to *create* is your greatest faculty. Everything that exists in your reality originated as a thought before it moved into the physical realm. The process your mind uses to do this is first to conceptualize; then visualize, affirming and re-affirming until belief sets in; it then interprets information in its environment to support that belief; and finally it manifests the result of the original thought.

Thought is the cause and the experience of your personal reality is the result. The quality of thought you entertain determines the quality of your reality. It is your attitude of mind toward life that determines the experiences that you encounter. If you expect nothing, you will receive nothing. If you demand abundance, you will receive the greater portion.

Thoughts are communicated through words. We all talk to ourselves constantly. The most important words you will ever speak are the words which you say to yourself.

What are you saying to yourself?

Words, like thoughts, are very powerful things. Choose your words carefully. Choose words that are in harmony with what you want for yourself. If the words you speak are in harmony with what you want, you will have harmony in your life.

Let go of the language that does not make you strong.

An effective way to do this is with the use of affirmations. An affirmation is a consciously chosen set of words that supports what you want for yourself.

Affirmations can be simple but powerful. They can change who you are. They can erase old programming and replace it with new ideas, with a new self-image, with new thought patterns, new beliefs and a new you!

If you want more in your life, you should affirm more.

One of the strongest affirmations which you can use for the purpose of strengthening your will and realizing your power to accomplish is;

"I CAN BE WHAT I WILL TO BE."

Every time you repeat this affirmation, think about who you really are; try to come to an understanding of your own true and divine nature. If you do, you will become invincible.

Affirm anything you want. Keep it simple and basic to start with and then build on it until you have created an entirely new picture of who you are.

CHAPTER THREE

THE POWER OF THE SUBCONSCIOUS

The subconscious processes are continually at work. We can learn to direct this work instead of being mere passive recipients of its activity. Some studies have shown that at least 90% of our mental activity is subconscious. If you do not learn to make use of this mental power, then you are narrowly limiting your mental activity.

What you are today is the direct result of your past thinking.

Your future self will be the direct result of your present thinking.

You can demand more out of life. You can consciously direct the events of your life rather than being merely a passive recipient of your life's activities.

Focus daily on what you want in your life.

Affirm the reality of what you desire.

Concentrate on what you want to become.

Demand more out of life.

Create your own reality by conscious intention. Affirm its reality until belief sets in. Idealize your desire and expect its manifestation. It will show up.

Plant the seed and expect the fruit. Know that it will come about because that is the natural process. It is the natural flow from the unseen into the seen, from vision into reality.

There is a great source of power within us. Circumstances present opportunities and needs, but the insight, strength, and power to address these needs and opportunities are found within us.

The power is from within but we cannot access this power unless we are willing to give it. Use is the condition upon which we hold this power.

And the more we give, the more we get.

Jesus taught a valuable truth in the parable of the talents. The financier who wishes to make money must make use of the money he has. Only by using what he has can he get more.

The athlete who wishes to get strong must make use of the strength he already has, and the more he gives, the more he gets.

Additional power is contingent upon the proper use of the power we already possess.

Nothing that can be thought of is ever truly impossible. Thought directs consciousness.

THINK CAREFULLY. THINK CLEARLY. THINK CONSCIOUSLY.

If your thoughts are harmonious, you create pleasant conditions. If your thoughts are discordant, you create uncomfortable conditions.

If your thoughts are in harmony with what you want, you will have harmony in your life. If they are not, your outer world will reflect the inharmonious conditions of your inner world.

The subconscious cannot reason. It takes you at your word. You have asked for something; you are now to receive it.

Every one of us talks to himself or herself all day long. Self-talk is a continuous, on-going activity of the mind. Pay attention to what you are telling yourself. Identify the self-talk that is not in harmony with what you want to create for yourself and then replace it with better thoughts and improved language.

Selecting a better language for your self-talk is accomplished through affirmation. Affirmation will replace negative thoughts. It will redirect random mental

"HAPPINESS DOES NOT DEPEND ON WHAT HAPPENS OUTSIDE OF YOU...BUT WHAT HAPPENS INSIDE OF YOU."

– HAROLD B. LEE

chatter and it can erase old mental programming tapes that run incessantly through our minds.

An affirmation is a consciously chosen set of words that support what you want for yourself.

Affirmations can change who you are. Affirmations will allow you to create new ideas, a new self-image, new and improved thought patterns, new beliefs and a new you.

If you want more in your life, you need to affirm more for yourself.

An affirmation can be very simple. Repeating *"I am loving"* to yourself over and over will make you into a more loving person much quicker than trying to remember to perform loving acts. The loving actions will follow and flow naturally as a result of your improved and empowered thought process.

You can affirm anything you want.

THE MOST IMPORTANT THINGS YOU SAY IN ANY GIVEN MOMENT ARE THE THINGS YOU SAY TO YOURSELF.

Your affirmations should be simple to begin with. You can then build on them until you have created an entirely new image of who you are.

The way to replace old mental programming running through your subconscious like an endlessly looping playback is through repeated affirmation. You can be what you will to be.

Exercise 3.1:

Create three simple affirmations that support the way you want to be, the things you want to do and the conditions you wish to create. Write them in your notebook. You can build on them later.

Start now to repeat those affirmations every day.

Through disciplined repetition of your supportive affirmations, these new thoughts will soon begin running through your subconscious process. They will then become the basis of a brand new belief system.

An empowering belief system will allow you to better visualize the conditions and circumstance you wish to create. Your ability to visualize what you want and to design your own life will become effortless.

There is an old saying: *"What you see is what you get."*

To manifest anything you want in life, you must first visualize it. The ideal you hold in your mind is the world you create around you.

The entire universe is an act of creative visualization. The same creative power, the power to visualize the life you desire, is within your grasp.

The process that leads to manifesting your desires begins with visualization.

There is a specific process of creativity. It is

1. Conceptualization.

2. Visualization.

3. Affirmation.

4. Belief.

5. Manifestation.

The first step is conceptualization. It is the most important step because it is the plan on which you are going to build. You must picture in your mind what it is that you want. You must be very clear and concise.

With every thought you are sowing seeds into your subconscious mind. As Kenneth Copeland stated, *"Every time we think, every time we feel, every time we exercise our will—we are sowing."* You need to be certain of what you want to harvest before you begin to randomly scatter those seeds.

The act of conceptualization is the art of picking the right seeds to produce the harvest for which you are hoping.

"Hold the vision, trust the process."

– Author Unknown

It is your ability to conceptualize and then visualize what you want that creates your reality. If you can conceptualize something, the potential exists for its manifestation.

If you can see it as real, it is real. The rest is technique, habit and application. The actual manifestation does not require effort. It will happen.

When you have the concept of what you desire, then visualize that desire.

You need to see where you are going. If you have no vision as to the direction of your life, you will end up stumbling around in the dark.

Illuminate the path toward your future using creative visualization. Nothing exists down that path except what you can see ahead of you and what you see ahead of you is a conscious choice. You actually create every detail, every circumstance of your future by your present visionary ability.

If you allow the previous programming of your subconscious mind to continue to dictate your circumstances, you will continue to be controlled. If, on the other hand, you wish to be in control of your life and your future, then you must consciously visualize exactly what you want to have happen.

Visualization is the process of making mental images. The image is the mold or model which will serve as the pattern from which your future will emerge.

Make the pattern clear and make it beautiful. Do not be afraid. No limitation can be placed upon you by anyone but yourself.

Construct your future, your new life, in your imagination. It will have to be built there before it will appear anywhere else.

Visualization takes practice but, with practice, you can become very good at it. Start out simple.

Exercise 3.2:

Practice by visualizing things that already exist.

Visualize your favorite coffee cup or a flower or the face of a loved one. Close your eyes and imagine one of these items or any other item familiar to you.

Close your eyes and visualize the color red.

Now visualize that color as a red rose.

Visualize the sun shining on its petals.

Visualize the folds in its petals.

Smell its fragrance.

Turn it around in your mind so that you see all sides of it.

Your thought is the cause;
THE EVENTS AND
CIRCUMSTANCES OF YOUR LIFE
ARE SIMPLY THE EFFECT.

When you are comfortable with visualizing objects that already exist, start creating new objects in your imagination. Remember, this is not the same as daydreaming. This is concentrated image creation. This is the creative act of visualization. Your imagination expands to the possibility of actually seeing the object as real.

Everything that exists in your world began in this same way. First as an idea, then as an image held in the mind of its creator.

This is also your power to create the objects and circumstances of the life you desire.

You construct the model of your future; you shape the mold from which your reality will emerge. You can make it as grand and as beautiful as you like. No one but you can place any limitation on the world you wish to create.

See the picture of what you wish to create in greater and greater detail every time you visualize. As you see these details in your imagination, you will begin to notice their manifestation.

EARNEST DESIRE WILL BRING CONFIDENT EXPECTATION.

Make the mental image. Make it clear, distinct, perfect. Hold it firmly. The ways and means will develop.

The process of manifestation has now begun in your mind and you need only follow it through to its conclusion.

There are many who have come to an understanding of this wonderful power, and who make serious and conscientious effort to realize health, abundance, power or other conditions, and yet seem to fail. They seem unable to bring the Law of Attraction into operation. The difficulty in nearly every case is that they are dealing with externals. They want money, power, health and abundance, but they fail to realize that these are only effects. Effects can only be created when we identify their cause.

By creating ideals only and giving no thought to external conditions, we create a beautiful and opulent world within and that inner world will manifest the same conditions in our outer surroundings. You will come to recognize your own personal power to create ideals and these ideals, in turn, will be projected into the world of effects.

Concentrate on things you want and not on things you do not want.

If you desire abundance, then idealize the methods and plans for putting the Law of Abundance into operation. Visualize the exact condition which the Law of Abundance creates; this will then result in manifestation.

See yourself being, doing and having everything you can imagine or conceptualize. Make it real. Make it complete and perfect in every detail and it will happen.

Plant your empowering seeds of thought into a field of pure potentiality and the process of materialization will take place as the result of natural law.

CHAPTER FOUR

THE POWER OF CHANGE

We all want more.

It is our nature to want more. We don't all necessarily want more of the same things; some may want more peace, others more love, others want better health, some want more money but we all want more.

So how do you get more?

We acquire more by becoming more.

The rule is; be more, do more, have more.

We never become more by having more. We have more by becoming more.

So how do we become more?

We become more by acquiring greater knowledge then integrating that knowledge into our belief systems. When we then apply that knowledge to give more of who we are we produce greater results. As we grow, our growth produces results which produce more growth.

You are in control of this process. Through your method of thinking, your consciousness creates your world.

When you place yourself in harmony with the Law of Attraction you assist in bringing about the desirable conditions in your life. An application of this law is absolutely essential to those desiring to make permanent progress and change.

If you want to change your world, or any part of your world, you must first change yourself. If you wish to change any condition, you must change yourself.

You can accomplish this simply by changing the way you think. The techniques are so simple that anyone can do them. The only requirement is that you apply them.

Change your method of thinking by conscious choice.

Change your subconscious programming by repeated affirmation.

Change your view of life by concentrated creative visualization.

Believe in the outcome.

Be grateful. Gratitude is what activates your power to create.

If you are not entirely pleased with the way your life is now, then change. You have the choice to think your own thoughts. But remember, your choice of thoughts has consequences in your life.

You have the choice to believe whatever you decide to believe. But remember, your beliefs affect your lifestyle.

THE GREATEST DISCOVERY OF ALL TIME IS THE POWER OF THOUGHT.

You can choose your actions. But your actions always have consequences.

It is the Law of Cause and Effect. It is reaping what you sow. You are responsible for your entire reality.

Do you want a new, different reality? Do you want to produce different, better results in your life? The key is in the Power of Change.

The process is simple; the application requires effort.

Change your beliefs.

Change your thinking pattern.

Change your habits.

Change your self-talk.

Change your actions.

You will produce better results.

IF LIFE IS NOT AS PERFECT AS YOU WANT IT TO BE—THEN CHANGE.

Exercise 4.1:

What is your intention in thinking what you think?

Are your thoughts supportive of your desires?

What results have your methods of thinking produced in your life?

Write your answers in your notebook.

Everything we get comes to us by the Law of Attraction. A happy thought cannot exist in an unhappy consciousness. Therefore, the consciousness must change and, as the consciousness changes, all conditions necessary to meet the changed consciousness must gradually change in order to meet the requirements of the new situation.

When we create a mental image or an ideal, we are projecting a thought into the mind from which our world is created.

Every day you think about 50,000 thoughts. 50,000 times a day you think something and your thoughts weave the cloth of your world.

Examine those thoughts. Are they constructive to what you want? Are they supportive of your ideals? Are they a harmonious flow of creative energy?

If not, then change your thoughts!

You have the power to choose and control your thoughts. Affirm what you want in your life. Focus on your ideal world. You are at cause. You create the effects of your life.

Your choices are the personal expression of your freewill (as we discussed in Chapter One of this book) and your choices determine your reality. You choose to believe something and then you choose to interpret the information received by your senses as supporting this belief. You can at any time choose to believe something else, something new, something different. As soon as you choose a new belief, all the evidence you receive will support that new belief.

Change your mind and you change your reality. Change your thoughts and you change the image of who you are.

Choose bigger. Choose better. Choose more.

Hold in mind the image you desire and it will become your reality.

What is your intentional thinking? Is it producing the results that you want?

Choose carefully what you think for *as we think, so are we.*

If you examine each circumstance and condition of your life, you will see clearly that the outer image of your reality is simply a reflection of the inner workings of your consciousness. The world without is a reflection of the world within.

Any train of thought persisted in will produce results on your character and your circumstances.

CHANGE YOUR MIND AND YOU CHANGE YOUR WORLD.

Exercise 4.2:

Look at some of the circumstances or characteristics of your life that you are unhappy with. Identify the persistent thoughts that have created these circumstances for you.

Write those thoughts in your notebook.

Now examine circumstances or characteristics of your life that you are pleased with. Identify the persistent thoughts that have created these circumstances for you.

Write these thoughts in your notebook.

You cannot directly choose your circumstances but you can choose your thoughts and by doing so shape your character and your circumstances.

To change the world around you, you have simply to change the world within you.

CHAPTER FIVE

THE POWER TO CREATE

The most apparent natural characteristic of the universe is growth. Stars die and are replaced by new stars. New stars are born every day. Cells die and are replaced by new cells. Growth runs rampant. Our universe is always becoming more.

The world itself was once void and without form. But matter formed and life showed up and now the earth produces more constantly. People and plants and animals are in a constant state of reproduction and growth.

And now you have arrived on the scene. So what happens next?

Creation is not a done deal. It is a constant flow of more.

You are the same.

If you were not constantly moving forward, growing new cells, processing foods, breathing air, pumping blood cells, you would not survive a single day. You are always becoming more. You are always in a state of growth.

Life is about growth. Growth is about change. Because of this, creation is a continuous and constant unfolding event.

So what happens next is entirely up to you. Your choices are infinite. You can be, do or have anything you desire. You need only awaken your consciousness, realize your potential and accept your Power to Create.

Your power to think is unlimited, consequently, your creative power is also unlimited.

The principle which gives thought the dynamic power to correlate with its object, and therefore master every adverse human experience is the Law of Attraction. As we mentioned in Chapter One, the Law of Attraction is simply another name for the Principle of Love.

This is an eternal and fundamental principle inherent in all things. Feeling imparts vitality to thought. Feeling is desire and desire is love. A thought infused with love becomes invincible.

Objects and conditions are created in the mental world before they appear as an event or an act in the outer world. By the simple process of governing our thought forces today, we create the events which will come into our lives in the future, perhaps even as early as tomorrow.

All mental discovery and attainment are the result of desire plus concentration. Desire is the strongest motive to action. The more persistent the desire, the more authoritative the revelation.

It is the combination of love and thought which creates the irresistible force known as the Law of Attraction.

If you concentrate on some matter of importance, your creative power of intuition will be set in operation.

Intuition can arrive at conclusions without the aid of experience or memory. Intuition can solve problems that are beyond the grasp of reasoning power.

And intuition can be cultivated and developed. Fundamentally, the subconscious is omnipotent. There is no limit to the things that can be done when the subconscious is given the desire to act.

Your degree of success in changing your world is determined by the nature of your desire. By keeping the thought of what you want to create in mind, it will gradually take tangible form. A definite purpose sets causes in motion which extend into the invisible world to attract the material necessary to create your purpose.

If you wish to eliminate fear, concentrate on courage.

If you wish to eliminate lack, concentrate on abundance.

"IMAGINATION IS MORE

IMPORTANT THAN

KNOWLEDGE."

– ALBERT EINSTEIN

If you wish to eliminate disease, concentrate on health.

Always concentrate on the ideal as an already existing fact.

Think certain thoughts and you will attract the necessary elements to produce a tangible reality.

You can assist the rate of your growth by being willing to let go of past limitations, past experiences, past pains and past resentments. A seed does not sprout until it lets go of the safety of its shell. It does not grow unless it releases the safety of being in the ground. It reaches out into the soil, sun and air, then blossoms and produces.

Like the seed, you need to release the restrictions of your limiting beliefs, thought patterns, habits and behaviors in order to grow. Let go of fear and anger and pain. Let go of the safety of your shell. Be willing to become more. Open yourself up to growth. Accept more.

Accept more love, accept more abilities, and accept more abundance, intelligence and growth. You are limited only by your imagination. You can be what you will to be. You can be what you choose to be.

Difficulties, disharmonies and obstacles in life indicate that we are holding on to what we no longer need. We are holding on to useless and worn-out materials. Choose to be willing to let go, to release, to forgive the past in order to grow and become more.

All things come through recognition. The scepter of power is consciousness; thought is its messenger and this messenger is constantly molding the realities of the invisible world into the conditions and environments of your objective world.

Thinking is the true business of life and power is the result. You are constantly and continuously dealing with the creative power of thought and consciousness. Visualization is your most powerful tool and imagination is your workshop.

Thought is creative and the quality of the conditions you create will depend on the quality of your thoughts. Every time you think you start a train of causation which will create a condition in strict accordance with the quality of the thought that originated it.

Some call this karma.

Others call it cause and effect.

Still others think of it as reaping what you sow.

But it is all the same.

Your thoughts produce results. You are at cause and you produce effects. Your creative power lies in your method of thinking.

Think the kind of thoughts that produce the results you are willing to claim as your own.

CHAPTER SIX

THE POWER OF GRATITUDE

Grateful appreciation in advance for your goals being accomplished is the best trick you can play on your mind. Gratitude proves to your subconscious that it had better catch up quickly to your reality. If you are thankful for having something, it will show up in your life.

You should be grateful for everything you have in life. Say thank you for each breath. This is one of your best affirmations.

How much would you be willing to pay for sunshine, for rain, for your child's love, for sleep, for hands and feet that work, and for each and every new day if all of these gifts and so much more had not been freely given to you?

How often do you pause to give thanks for these everyday things? How often is your heart suffused with amazement and gratitude for the magnificence of life's greatest gifts?

We so often thoughtlessly and obtusely take it all so easily for granted.

"Gratitude," Samuel Johnson said over two centuries ago, *"is a fruit of great cultivation; it is not found among uncultured people."* This being the case, a vital objective in our determination toward becoming more should be the development of an active and *constant* attitude of gratitude.

Gratefulness is a wholesome and honorable quality of character. A consciousness bathed in the light of gratitude and thanksgiving sees itself and the rest of the world in authentic terms. In the light of gratitude, there can be no egotistical self-sufficiency.

Based on what we have learned so far, if you are grateful for anything in your life, you might as well be grateful for everything, since all events, circumstances and conditions you have undergone were necessary to bring you to where you are now.

Exercise 6.1:

In your notebook make a list of ten things in your life that you are grateful for.

Now make a list in your notebook of ten things you are grateful for that you are hoping will show up in your life.

"What would you not pay to see the moon rise if nature had not made it free entertainment?"

– Richard Le Gallienne

Look at our galaxy. It contains billions of suns and billions of planets. And within our universe there are billions of galaxies.

There is an apparent infinite potential to our universe.

Lack and limitation do not exist in nature.

Abundance, bounty and plenty exist everywhere.

Creation is the calling into existence of that which does not exist in the objective world.

Everywhere in creation, abundance is the rule. The natural flow of the universe is toward increased abundance. Otherwise, there would be no universe.

Look at nature and you will see natural law and the natural order of growth. One seed sprouts, blossoms and engenders more seeds which multiply into more and more seeds. Trillions and trillions of hydrogen molecules fire our sun and new suns are constantly being created.

SEE AND ACCEPT ALL

OCCURRENCES AS

SUCCESSFUL STEPS ON YOUR

PATH TO SUCCESS.

You also began one day as a single cell, then became two, and then millions more. You replace old dying cells with new cells every day. Abundance runs rampant within you.

So why do humans suffer lack and limitation?

Scarcity and limitation are a historical fact in the human experience.

Power comes from within. Every lack, limitation or adverse circumstance is the result of weakness. Weakness is simply the absence of power. Wisdom, strength and courage and all harmonious conditions are the result of power. The remedy is to develop more and greater power.

Our choices determine our abundance. We can choose to have more by choosing to be more.

Be more. Do more. Have more.

Your consciousness is similar to a garden. Your garden may be intelligently plowed and planted or it can

INGRATITUDE IS ONE OF THE GREATEST SETBACKS ON OUR PATH TO SUCCESS.

be neglected and left to run wild; but whether cultivated or neglected, it must and will produce.

If you fail to purposefully plant useful seeds in the soil of your mind, then an abundance of useless thoughts, like the seeds of a dandelion, will find their way into your consciousness, sprouting and producing useless acts, events and circumstances.

Your method of thinking, your consciousness, creates your world. Gratitude is a thought pattern strongly tied to an emotion and it will take root, blossoming eventually into acts, events and circumstances that will bear the fruit of opportunity and abundance.

In order to possess the vitality necessary to produce results, thought must be permeated with desire. Desire is a form of love and love imparts vitality to thought and enables it to grow. Gratitude is one of the deepest expressions of love.

Appreciation is a beneficial feeling with a peculiar therapeutic power. But gratitude easily slips away from us. If we don't look deep into ourselves and admit how much we need the power gratitude releases, not just during a day, a month, or a season, but throughout our lives, then we lose the benefit that being thankful brings to us.

Gratitude releases a particular psychodynamic energy. It helps us focus on the positive and draws us away from the negative. This process generates optimism and self-confidence. It also draws our attention away from destructive self-centeredness and opens us to doing more for others. We feel impelled to repay kindness with kindness, service with service, and trust with trust. Human barriers are broken, and emotional horizons pushed back.

Gratitude is also a principle that should be cultivated by unhappy individuals. The best way to counter anger and frustration when things go wrong is to remember all the times when things went right. That is gratitude's hidden, healing power. Our challenge is to make it a permanent part of our conscious development.

Sincere gratitude is conveyed through our actions more than simply through our words. Being grateful means giving a fullness of thanks. Giving thanks is the outward expression of a grateful heart. Gratitude is the feeling within our hearts.

Thankfulness is quantified by the expression of our words; gratitude is gauged by the nature of our actions. Thankfulness is the beginning of gratitude; gratitude the completion of thankfulness. It is infinitely more efficient to accept all things with gratitude and view them as contributing to your success.

When you focus constantly on the beneficial aspects of life, you are bound to benefit as a result. A willing compliance with natural law enables us to engender permanent positive growth. Resistance to negativity only serves to attract more negativity.

Thought will create conditions in accordance with the predominant mental attitude.

If we fear disaster, disaster will be a certain result of our thinking.

SUCCESS IS CREATED BY HARMONY.

Everything we receive comes by the Law of Attraction. In expressing gratitude for what we don't have but desire to have, we are projecting a thought that can bring about the realization of our desire.

Our subconscious does not take into consideration time or space. It can only comprehend the present moment. It is important to affirm and visualize goals as already completed in the present. It is equally important to be grateful for those things you desire even before you have received them.

While the subconscious acts without our knowledge, we have learned that the subconscious mind is responsive to the conscious mind. The conscious mind can purposefully suggest thoughts which the subconscious mind will put into action.

Thought is the reality. Conditions are merely the outward manifestations of thought. As thought changes, all outward manifestations or material conditions must change to stay in harmony with the new thoughts.

Harmonize your thoughts with natural law and you will be enriched.

All conditions and experiences that manifest in our lives come to us for our benefit and growth. Difficulties and obstacles will continue to come until we absorb their wisdom and gather from them the essentials for further growth.

The law is that we reap what we sow.

Honest gratitude implies more than just a feeling of the heart. It implies more than merely a vocal or written expression of thanks. Sincere gratitude implies action. Gratefulness literally implies demonstrating thanks by giving.

We demonstrate heart-felt gratitude through offering kind gestures, listening ears, open hearts to anyone in need. In this way, we are not simply *giving* thanks, we are offering *living* thanks. Anne Morrow Lindbergh said it this way: *"One can never pay in gratitude; one can only pay 'in kind' somewhere else in life."*

In a similar fashion, if we are thankful for the treasures of strength, abundance and ability that enrich our lives, we should show gratitude by not hording these precious treasures in our hearts where we alone benefit from them. We should share them with others.

To be filled with gratitude is one of the most important principles for receiving the manifestation of our desires. We should give thanks for whatever gifts have been manifested in our lives up to this point. When we receive all things with thankfulness, we put ourselves into a position to receive even more, for which we should be even more grateful.

When we develop a sincere expression of gratitude for all that we have been given, we are, in effect, opening up the channels to receive even more. If we are grateful for what we already have, we will receive more.

It is not possible to overdo gratitude.

Exercise 6.2:

Examine some of the hardships and trials you have gone through in your life.

Identify the growth of character and valuable lessons you have learned from them.

List these in your notebook.

Express sincere gratitude for the benefit you have received from the difficult experiences you have encountered.

CHAPTER SEVEN

PROSPERITY CONSCIOUSNESS

What is wealth?

Think carefully.

Wealth is not the accumulation of money or things. Wealth is not based on possession.

True wealth is not about having more stuff. Stuff is fleeting, Stuff is effects. Stuff does not fulfill the desire to become more or to grow into what we know we can become.

True wealth is about being abundantly able to contribute more. True wealth is about creative freedom.

Most of us think of wealth as being manifest in having things but that is a hollow wealth unless having it empowers us with a greater ability to give, to contribute, and to engender wealth in others.

True wealth is being more in order to contribute more. As a result, we will automatically have more.

Studies have shown that lottery winners who have won over a million dollars are, within five years, farther in debt than before they won. This is because they never became more and never did more. We must be more in order to have more. We become more by being of service in bigger and better ways.

Wealth is the effect of the consciousness. It is a willingness to be more. Allowing is the cause. Wealth is the effect.

Wealth is a product of labor. Capital is an effect, not a cause. Wealth is a servant, not a master. Money is a means, not an end.

Wealth should not be desired as the end result but simply as a means of accomplishing an end.

Everything in the universe is about growth, change and flow. Wealth flows through you and you are simply a channel of distribution. The more willing you are to contribute and give, the more you are open to receive.

This is true of everything. If you want more love, give more love; if you want more respect, be more respectful; if you want more prosperity, become more giving. You open up the channel of receiving by giving more.

We are all familiar with the Law of Sowing and Reaping. Ask any farmer; the more you sow, the more you reap; and it is always more. One wheat kernel planted yields almost a hundred new kernels.

Every thought, every emotion, every word spoken, every action on your part is a seed sown. Examine your thoughts, feelings and actions and you will discover what your harvest will be. What are you sowing? What will your harvest be?

All of us are constantly sowing seeds. In order to reap the things that we want, we need only figure out how to first sow those same things.

You will find that the more you give, the more you will get. Giving in this sense implies service. The banker gives money, the merchant gives goods, the author gives thoughts and ideas, and the laborer gives skill. We all have something to give and the more we can give, the more we will get. The more we get, the more we are enabled to give.

Success is contingent on an ideal higher than the mere accumulation of riches. Those who aspire to such success must formulate an ideal for which they are willing to strive. With such an ideal in mind, the ways and means can and will be provided.

Our success depends on our creative ability. The Power to Create depends entirely on our spiritual power. The three creative steps, as we discussed earlier are idealization, visualization, and materialization.

We can form our own mental images, through our own interior process of thought, regardless of what others think, regardless of exterior conditions, regardless of environment of any kind. It is by the exercise of this power that we control our own destiny.

It is by the exercise of this power that we take our fate out of the hands of chance and consciously make for ourselves the experiences which we desire. To control thought is to control circumstances, conditions, environment and destiny. If our thought is harmonious and constructive we will manifest good. If it is destructive and discordant, we will manifest evil.

If you desire to visualize a different environment, the process is simply to hold the ideal in mind, until your vision has been made real. This is an exact scientific fact.

What we think determines the quality of our mind and the quality of our mind determines our ability and mental capability. The improvement in our ability will naturally be followed by increase in our attainment and a greater control of our circumstances.

THE FIRST LAW OF SUCCESS IS SERVICE.

Form a mental picture of success in your mind by consciously visualizing your desire. In this way you will be compelling success. You will be attracting success into your life.

Creative thinking requires attention. The Power of Attention is called *concentration*. This power is directed by the will. For this reason we must refuse to concentrate or think of anything except the things we desire.

Wealth is our birthright. We may choose to claim any or all of it as our own. We have the freedom of choice. All we need is the willingness to accept more.

Wealth is demonstrated by giving and by being of service.

Service means being ready, willing and able to give, to contribute and to make a difference. You are enabled to give more by becoming more. The natural flow is be more, do more, have more. If you want to have more, you need to do more. In order to do more, you need to become more.

Concentrate on being more than you are now. How do you become more? Give more. Give more to yourself and give more to others.

Find a way to create for others what you want for yourself and you will receive more. If you want wealth, help others become wealthy.

"You can get anything you want if you will only help enough other people get what they want."

The wealthiest people in the world did not get wealthy because they lost money for other people. On the contrary, it is because they made money for other people that they became the wealthiest people on the planet.

Prosperity consciousness is built upon the recognition that there is no lack. There is no limitation. There is no need to compete with others because there is an abundance of supply.

If you want more money, find out how to make more money for others. Money is simply an exchange of energy. A dollar bill has no inherent value other than an exchange value. What value are you willing to give in order to receive cash in return?

Many spiritually minded people cannot resolve the dilemma of material wealth. Many materialistic people ignore the spiritual aspects of their lives. How can we desire material riches and still be spiritually focused?

Consider the fact that you are not a human being with a spirit but are, rather, a spiritual being with a body. Being spiritual, your desires are incapable of any permanent satisfaction in anything that is not spiritual. Money is of no value except to bring about the conditions which you desire.

You can be spiritual and still desire wealth and abundance.

Money consciousness involves an understanding of value; *your* value. Become valuable and you will receive valuables.

Decide what you have to offer to others in return for money and then be prepared to give more value than asked for and money will flow to you.

Money consciousness is an attitude of the mind.

Any marketer will tell you we make money by making friends. We enlarge our circle of friends by making money for them, by helping them, by being of service to them.

Prosperity is cash flow. You will stop the inbound flow if you stop the outbound flow.

Money consciousness is about having a receptive attitude. Desire is the attractive force which sets the current in motion. Fear is the obstacle that stops the current. Fear is poverty consciousness. We get exactly what we give. If we give fear, we receive what is feared.

The real secret behind becoming wealthy is learning how to create wealth. Become abundant. Become a blessing to someone and you will be blessed in return.

All wealth originates in thought. Thought is the only activity of consciousness. Your ability to think is your ability to create wealth.

You may choose to create wealth, abundance and plenty in any area of your life.

Would you like more love? Be more loving.

Would you like greater health? Become more alive.

Would you like more wealth? Become more abundant.

Would you like to receive more? Be more giving.

Cash flow is like the flow of a stream. You can reach in for a handful to quench your thirst or you can dip a cup into the stream to get more. You can take a bucketful or you can build a reservoir. You can get as wet and as wealthy as you like.

You decide. The abundance is always there and always flowing passed you.

Make a commitment to change and to grow and you will be showered with plenty.

Be of service and you will attain wealth.

CHAPTER EIGHT

HEALTH CONSCIOUSNESS

The body obeys the direction of the mind, whether those directions are deliberately chosen or simply random, automatic and habitual. If you want to improve your body's health, you need to guard your thoughts.

Our bodies are delicate and malleable mechanisms. They respond readily to the thoughts we impress on them.

True physical health and well-being are dependent upon emotional, mental and spiritual health. Any illness or physical discomfort is a specific signal that some aspect of our inner being needs attention and correction. Spiritual, emotional and mental illness creates physical dis-ease and dis-comfort.

Our method of thinking, in large part, determines our health. If you want greater health, become more health conscious. Thought is the source of action and manifestation.

Eliminating thoughts of fear, worry, care, anxiety, jealousy, hatred and every other destructive thought which tends to tear down and destroy our systems will increase the inflow and distribution of vital energy throughout our system.

Every time we have a thought we are producing chemicals called neuropeptides. These chemicals are part protein and part energy. They are the language of the brain, like thoughts in physical form.

There are receptors for these neuropeptides on various cells in the body that allow communication and information to be exchanged. Neuropeptides are the material-physical equivalent of thought.

Your immune system, a series a white blood cells, protects your body from foreign viruses, bacteria and fungus and performs many functions for your health and well-being.

The monocyte white blood cell has a receptor for every known neuropeptide.

Every atom of every cell in your body has intelligence, awareness and thought. You can't have an idea, thought, emotion or desire without your immune system knowing about it. The immune system is literally eavesdropping in on the conversation you are having with yourself.

The immune cells can make the same chemicals or neuropeptides that the brain and nervous system make the instant you have a thought. This implies that the immune cells are thinking, cognizant cells.

The immune system is like a circulating nervous system.

THE REAL BATTLE OF LIFE IS ONE OF IDEAS.

Think of a body part in distress. The first immune cell to arrive on the scene of distress is the monocyte. This is the one with the receptor for all known neuropeptides. What your body, in its infinite intelligence is doing, is sending to the distressed part of your body the very emotion, thought or feeling you may have been too protected to feel.

Every cell in the body is replaced at least every seven years. Some sources say every seven months to a year. So, if we have an injury to a body part or if we have a tumor, for example, it is not the same atoms, molecules or cells a year to seven years later. Our body is creating the same, less-than-perfect new cells because the picture being held in our conscious or subconscious is less than perfect. The cause is the thought, the mental image that is being predominantly entertained. The illness is the effect, the expression of the thought.

We are always either re-creating old patterns or dissolving these old patterns by changing our thoughts and mental images of who and what we think we are.

"Change of Diet will not help a man who will not change his thoughts."

– James Allen

Holding the perfect ideal in mind you can bring about the ideal conditions in your environment. If you see only the incomplete, the imperfect, the infirm, these conditions will manifest in your life.

If you want good health, think healthy thoughts.

Frederic Lehrman suggests the following revealing experiment from his popular seminars.

Find a quiet room with a comfortable chair. Sit with your back upright and your feet flat on the floor. Close your eyes and take a few minutes to relax. Quiet your mind.

Now, imagine yourself contracting a serious illness.

I can almost hear your reaction; "Are you crazy, Steven? I'm not going to do that!"

Good. Please DON'T DO THIS EXPERIMENT! Instead, think about why you had such an adverse reaction to even the suggestion of imagining yourself with a serious illness.

Is it because you are afraid it would work? Do you believe you could actually contract an illness simply by suggesting the possibility to your subconscious mind?

Now imagine that I had asked you to perform the same experiment but instead of imaging you have a serious illness, I had asked you to imagine that you are in perfect physical and mental health.

What would your reaction have been? If you are like most people you would have discounted the suggestion as absurd and ineffective.

Why is it that we trust our mind's ability to produce a negative effect in our lives simply by thinking about something negative, yet we so readily dismiss our conscious power to produce positive effects?

Illness and health are both deeply rooted in thought. In his book, *As a Man Thinketh*, James Allen explains that *"the people who live in fear of disease are the people who get it."* Unhealthy thoughts will manifest themselves through an unhealthy body. Healthy, wholesome and cheerful thoughts strengthen the body in energy and elegance.

Quoting James Allen again, *"There is no physician like cheerful thought."*

CHAPTER NINE

YOUR SECRET POWER

The universe is governed by law. One of those laws states that for every effect there must be a cause and that the same cause, under the same conditions, will invariably produce the same effect.

As we become conscious of the inexhaustible power of the world within our thoughts, we will begin to draw on this power and apply and develop the greater possibilities which this discernment has realized, because whatever we become conscious of is invariably manifested in the objective world and brought forth into tangible expression.

The real secret of power is consciousness of power.

Our ability to eliminate imperfect conditions depends upon mental action and mental action depends upon consciousness of power. The more conscious we become of our metal power, the greater will be our power to control and master every condition.

Our ability to think is our ability to act and what we think is what is created or produced in the objective world.

When we realize these facts concerning our thoughts we understand how we may bring to ourselves any condition by creating the corresponding conditions in our consciousness. Everything we hold in our consciousness for any length of time eventually becomes impressed upon the subconscious and thus becomes a pattern which our creative energy will weave into our life and environment.

The predominant thought or mental attitude is the magnet and the law is that like attracts like, consequently the mental attitude will invariably attract such conditions as correspond to its nature.

When you accept "response-ability" for who you are, you accept the *ability* to *respond* to the world around you. You have the ability to choose your thoughts and beliefs.

You have the choice.

You have the power.

You are at cause.

You can be what you choose to be.

You can become what you choose to think.

Thought is creative and thought is the power by which your world is transformed.

Thoughts of abundance will respond to similar thoughts.

"Everything is energy and that's all there is to it. Match the frequency of the reality you want and you cannot help but get that reality. It can be no other way. This is not philosophy. This is physics."

– Albert Einstein

Affluent thoughts are the secret of attraction for an affluent lifestyle. Your thoughts are the energy by which the Law of Attraction is brought into operation, which eventually manifests in abundance.

The use of this power depends upon *attention*. The degree of attention determines the capacity for acquiring power. Power depends upon the consciousness of power. Unless you use it, you will lose it and you cannot use it if you are not conscious of it.

Concentrate on your power to create.

The more you become, the more you can do. The more you do, the more you will have. Be more, do more, have more.

Accept "response-ability" for all things, events and circumstances in your life. Your consciousness creates your world.

All the fear, all the doubt, and all the uncertainties will gently dissolve as soon as you assume responsibility for being at cause.

"ANYTHING THE MIND OF MAN CAN CONCEIVE AND BELIEVE, IT CAN ACHIEVE."

- NAPOLEON HILL

You have the ability to create your own results, your own wealth, and your own effects. You are at cause and you produce effects.

You are responsible for everything you create. Your creative power is your method of thinking.

As we said earlier, think only those things which you are willing and able to claim as your own.

Your thoughts, intentions and desires are the ultimate cause of everything you go through. If it is not as perfect as you would like it to be, then change.

You have the power to affirm what you truly want. You have the power to visualize what you truly want. You have the power to be grateful for what you truly want.

This is a lifetime effort. The more you become, the more you are capable of becoming. Your potential is limitless. You can create anything you desire in life. Your only limitation is the arbitrary and self-imposed beliefs which you can choose to replace with empowering beliefs.

"WE ARE WHAT AND WHERE WE ARE BECAUSE WE HAVE FIRST IMAGINED IT."

– DONALD CURTIS

Your method of thinking controls what happens in your life and you choose every thought. You can program your mind though continuous affirmation to create the results you want in your life.

You can be more, and as a result you can do more. It is then that you will have more.

You can freely choose to be more, do more and have more. Whatever you choose, you are responsible.

If you see only the incomplete, the imperfect, the relative, the limited, then these conditions will manifest in your life.

If you want to experience abundance, you must think abundance. If you want to experience health, you must think health. If you want to experience harmony in any aspect of your life, you must think harmonious thoughts.

Your real work consists in convincing yourself of the truth of these statements.

Nothing can permanently stand in the way of your perfect success when you learn to apply the scientifically correct thought methods and principles.

Focus and concentrated thought is the true method of reaching, awakening and expressing the wonderful potential power of the world within you.

CHAPTER TEN

YOUR NEXT STEPS TO ACHIEVING POWER

There are seven clear, identifiable steps to success in any area of life. The following pages will enable you to be empowered to new and greater levels of personal power and accomplishment.

These are the seven steps:

1. Identify your potential.
2. Achieve clarity of purpose.
3. Focus your attention by setting goals.
4. Utilize proven techniques.

5. Believe and persist.

6. Be of service.

7. Be forgiving and grateful.

Be prepared to spend several hours, even days maybe, completing the exercises on the following pages.

1. Identify your potential.

It is necessary that you accept full and complete responsibility for where you find yourself right now. If you say it is because of your parents, or your lack of education or the economy, you are not taking responsibility. Your present reality, all of it—everything you have and see in your life at this moment, is the result of your past beliefs, thoughts, feelings and actions.

Any obstacles or limitations that you have identified as preventing you from achieving complete success are simply excuses. Once you take "response-ability," you realize that you have the power to create your future by choosing your beliefs, thoughts, feelings and actions.

Exercise 10.1:

Write down in your notebook what you *believe your true potential is.*

2. Clarity of purpose.

Think of your life five years from now.

What does it look like?

How does it feel?

What will have to happen to you to get you there?

Exercise 10.2:

Write down your thoughts about the above questions.

Now, slowly move back in time reviewing successive steps that you will accomplish to fulfill your purpose...3 years from now...1 year from now...6 months...1 month...one week...until you come to today.

"The journey of a thousand miles begins with a single step."

– Lao Tzu

What is the first step that you need to take to accomplish your purpose?

Write it down and commit to taking that first step today!

Think of a time when you were 100% successful. Think of something that you did; a task, an event or a challenge that you completed and you knew it was perfect.

Write down the essence of this event in your notebook.

Come to an understanding of what you did that resulted in your success. Remember, you are the one who did it! When you realize that your power, your happiness, your prosperity come from within you and recognize what it is that you did to attain the desired results, you can effortlessly recreate success in every area of your life.

"If you are upset by anything external, the pain is not due to that external thing, but to your own interpretation of it, and this you have the power to revoke at any moment."

– Marcus Aurelius

3. Focus your attention by setting goals.

In 1984 a study was conducted on the Harvard Business School graduating class of 1964.

Only 5% of the graduating class had taken the time and made the effort to write down their goals. Of this group, 95% had achieved their goals.

Of the 95% who did not have written goals in 1964, only 5% had achieved their expected goals over 20 years.

Having written goals is imperative. We succeed best when we plan to succeed.

A similar study was conducted at Yale University. Only 3% of the 1953 graduating class had written goals. Twenty years later it was found that this 3% had accomplished more than the other 97% of students combined.

What are your goals?

Are they written down?

Do you review them regularly?

When President Kennedy decided to put a man on the moon, fully 50% of the technology required to do so did not exist at the time. The decision to set the goal and believe in the possibility of its achievement produced the necessary scientific and technological innovations to make it possible.

When we decide to accomplish a goal in our lives, it is not necessary that we have the education, money, intelligence or tools to achieve the goal. It is only necessary to believe in our ability and persist in the direction of accomplishing that goal. All the necessary ingredients will come along to make it possible.

Remember that the subconscious does not take into consideration time or space. It can only comprehend NOW. Once you have identified your goals, it is important that you affirm and visualize them as already being present and already complete.

The first step is deciding what you want.

Write down the goals that seem most extraordinary for your life.

Exercise 10.3:

Ask yourself, "What do I want to achieve in each of the following areas of my life?"

Physical.

Mental.

Spiritual.

Social.

Emotional.

Financial.

What do I need in my life to feel successful?

What do I need to change to achieve that success?

What will I commit to do now instead of day-dreaming about it or regretting that I have never done it?

Re-think and re-write your goals in harmony with your chosen purpose. Write them in your notebook and on 3x5 cards that you can carry with you. Read them to yourself at least twice a day.

Your intentions will always equal your results. Be conscious of what your intentions are. Listen to your self-talk. Become aware of areas where you may be undermining your own success.

Continually ask yourself, *"What is my intention in thinking what I am thinking right now? Does it contribute to my success and fulfillment?"*

4. Utilize proven techniques.

By utilizing proven techniques to accomplish your goals, you will become more.

By identifying your goals and ambitions and being clear on where you are going, you will do more than you have ever done.

In order for any thing or event to be manifest in your reality, it first needs to be pictured in its entirety in your mind. When you visualize your ambitions, attach desire for their manifestation in your life. Your subconscious will provide the necessary mechanism to bring it about.

True visualization means being able to see as clearly in your mind as you can with your eyes.

Repeating affirmations is exactly like recording over an old tape. You are impressing upon your subconscious the new belief you wish to incorporate into your life. With affirmations, you can replace previous, non-productive beliefs, negative thoughts and feelings of low self-esteem with new, powerful, and productive beliefs.

Exercise 10.4:

Write down the first item from your goals list that you will visualize as being already accomplished.

"IT IS IN YOUR MOMENTS OF

DECISION THAT YOUR DESTINY

IS SHAPED."

– ANTHONY ROBBINS

Write down your personal favorite affirmations. Commit them to memory and repeat them every day.

5. Believe and persist.

Beliefs are the cornerstone to your accomplishment. Once you have the ideal in mind and have visualized it, you must believe that you have already achieved it. This is the key to all attainment.

Belief can be developed. Hold on to your vision and it will manifest itself.

Trust in your ability to create.

Exercise 10.5:

Write down some of your beliefs. Identify whether these beliefs empower you or hold you back.

Practice daily believing in yourself and believing in where you are going. Here are some suggestions:

Read your written goals at least twice a day.

Associate with people that support your goals and beliefs.

Daily visualize your goals as completed.

Write a list of affirmations that support the beliefs you need to succeed.

Persist! Do not let anyone steal your dream.

Persistence is belief in action. A child believes it can walk and it persists until it is successful. Your belief in your own success will ensure that you persist until you are successful. Do not be swayed by circumstance, conditions or the opinions of others.

We can often become distracted by the world. Keep track of those seemingly miraculous occurrences that will increase in frequency throughout your life.

6. Be of Service.

Service is not just the things that you do for others. Service is an attitude. What you give determines what you get. Always find a way to add value to who you are and what you do.

Where can you be of greater service?

Exercise 10.6:

Identify three areas where you can add service. Write them in your notebook.

Begin doing them now.

7. Gratitude and Forgiveness.

Grateful appreciation in advance is the best trick you can play on your subconscious mind.

"BELIEVE THAT LIFE IS WORTH LIVING AND YOUR BELIEF WILL CREATE THE FACT."

– WILLIAM JAMES

Exercise 10.7:

Review the list from your notebook of the things in your life that you are grateful for.

Now review your list of the things in your life that you have not yet received that you are grateful for.

Be truly grateful for all that you have and all that you are going to have.

Forgiveness is what sets you free. If you resent or regret anything or if you blame others for your circumstances or challenges in life, you are chained to fear and anger. Let it go and you will no longer be held back by past occurrences or by other negative people.

The three necessary stages of forgiveness are as follows.

1. Forgive yourself for all failures, shortcomings and weaknesses.
2. Forgive all others for any perceived slights, hurt or limitation that may have been inflicted on you.

3. Be grateful. Once you have forgiven, remember that everything that has happened to you was necessary to bring you to where you are now.

Exercise 10.7:

Make a list of the things you want to let go of or transform from failures to forgiveness?

Begin working on them now.

Conclusion.

Now that you have learned how to use the Power of Choice to influence your conscious and subconscious mind, you can use the Power of Attraction to eliminate what you don't want in your life and create and attract much more of what you do want in your life.

You are already a success at using the Power of Attraction. Now all you need is to use it deliberately and consciously for your benefit and improvement.

"I CHOOSE...

TO LIVE BY CHOICE, NOT BY CHANCE.

TO BE MOTIVATED, NOT MANIPULATED.

TO BE USEFUL, NOT USED.

TO MAKE CHANGES, NOT EXCUSES.

TO EXCEL, NOT COMPETE.

I CHOOSE SELF-ESTEEM, NOT SELF-PITY.

I CHOOSE TO LISTEN TO MY INNER VOICE, NOT THE RANDOM OPINIONS OF OTHERS."

www.ingramcontent.com/pod-product-compliance
Lightning Source LLC
Chambersburg PA
CBHW052010090426

42741CB00008B/1632